Defenders of the Faith
Winning the War

Jason Fros'T Neville

Defenders of the Faith: Winning the War

Copyright © 2023 PCCF

For more information, please contact:

Jason Neville
Praise Chapel Christian Fellowship
3034 E Gage Ave
Huntington Park, Ca 90255
(323) 589-8957
(562) 254-5498
www.praisechapelcf.com

Published by Praise Publications
All rights reserved printed in the United States of America

Table of Contents

Dedicated to My Wife and Kids

My first book, "Defenders of the Faith, Winning the War", is dedicated to my personal Defenders of the Faith: Jackie, my wonderful and beautiful wife of 26 years; and my 3 children Michael, Jake, Kalina, and my son-in-law Daryl. Thank you for always standing with me as I have defended the faith. You've always encouraged me to do what God has called me to do, and for that, I am grateful. My prayer is that as previous generations have impacted my life, you all will continue the legacy, standing to defend the faith. My joy will be complete knowing that this same legacy of faith will be passed on to my grandchildren and great-grandchildren.

I love you,

Your loving husband and father

Introduction
"Defenders of the Faith, Winning The War"

War stories. Who doesn't like them? My grandfather served our country in the military and fought in the wars. As a kid, I remember him telling me stories about the battles he had been engaged in. I always thought to myself how incredibly, heroic, and courageous these soldiers must have been to be on the frontlines of a raging war.

Like many of you, I am a boxing fan and learned that there is a difference between losing a round and losing the fight. In Rocky V, starring Sylvester Stallone as Rocky, there's a scene where Rocky and an up-and-coming boxer named Tommy Gun get into a fight in the alley. Rocky was on the losing end of this fight when he was knocked down. Tommy, thinking he had beaten Rocky, turned, and started to walk away. That's when Rocky got up and said, "Hey Yo Tommy, I didn't hear no bell, where you are going." Obviously Rocky is telling Tommy he has more fight left in him and it wasn't over. It's been said, it ain't over until it's over.

This book is saying the same thing to you: Hey Yo, Christ follower. God has a great plan for your life. He desires to prosper you and give you a future. However, it won't come without a fight.

As Defenders of the Faith, we are in a spiritual war, with a target on our backs, because we represent a threat to the kingdom of darkness. The Bible is clear about this war in Ephesians 6:12; "For we are not fighting against flesh-and-blood enemies, but against evil rulers and authorities of the unseen world, against mighty powers in this dark world, and against evil spirits in the heavenly places.

The Apostle Paul goes on to say in 2 Corinthians 10:3-5; For though we live in the world, we do not wage war as the world does. The weapons we fight with are not the weapons of the world. On the contrary, they have divine power to demolish strongholds. We demolish arguments and every pretension that sets itself up against the knowledge of God, and we take captive every thought to make it obedient to Christ.

In 1 Timothy 6:12, Paul exhorts Timothy to fight the good fight of the faith. Take hold of the eternal life to which you were called when you made your good confession in the presence of many witnesses. The reason it's called a good fight is because we win!

As Defenders of the Faith, we are on the frontlines of the war and are to preach the word; win the lost; heal the sick; and cast out demons. In order to accomplish this, we are to put on the full armor of God: Ephesians 6:11-17; Put on the full armor of God, so that you can take your stand against the devil's schemes. For our struggle is not against flesh and blood, but against the rulers, against the authorities, against the powers of this dark world, and against the spiritual forces of evil in the heavenly realms. Therefore, put on the full armor of God, so that when the day of evil comes, you may be able to stand your ground, and after you have done everything, to stand. Stand firm then, with the belt of truth buckled around your waist, with the breastplate of righteousness in place, and with your feet fitted with the readiness that comes from the gospel of peace. In addition to all this, take up the shield of faith, with which you can extinguish all the flaming arrows of the evil one. Take the helmet of salvation and the sword of the Spirit, which is the word of God.

As you move into the role of a Defender of the Faith, always remember that you'll be challenged to give up and quit. But don't do it. You have everything you need to accomplish your task. Cast your care on Jesus, humble yourself before Him and He will give you the victory.

Remember, losing a few rounds doesn't mean you've lost the battle. Keep moving forward in what you've been taught, and watch God bring the victory.

From one Defender of the Faith to another ...let's win the war.

Jason Neville

CHAPTER 1

Be Ready to Share God's Word

"Preach the word; be ready in season and out of season;
reprove, rebuke, and exhort with complete
patience and teaching."
2 Timothy 4:2 (ESV)

As **Defenders of the Faith,** we must always be ready to preach the Word of God, even when it is not convenient.

As Christ followers, we are called to always be ready to proclaim the truth of God's Word to those around us. The apostle Paul, in his letter to Timothy, emphasizes the importance of being prepared to preach and teach the Scriptures. In 2 Timothy 4:2, he urges Timothy to "preach the word; be ready in season and out of season."

To be ready in season and out of season means that our commitment to sharing God's Word should not waver based on our circumstances or the response we receive. It requires dedication and a deep conviction in the power of God's Word to transform lives. We are called to faithfully proclaim the truth, regardless of whether it is convenient or popular.

Being ready also requires preparedness. Just as an athlete trains before a competition or a musician practices diligently before a performance, we too must invest time and effort in studying and understanding God's Word. We cannot effectively share what we do not know. We need to immerse ourselves in the Scriptures, allowing them to shape our hearts and minds so that we can communicate their truth with clarity and conviction.

As we seek to be ready to share God's Word, three key points are made from this verse: reprove, rebuke, and exhort. Let's take a look:

1. Reprove: The Word of God convicts and exposes sin in our lives. It shines a light on areas that need correction and prompts us to repent. When we share God's Word, we should not shy away from confronting sin and calling others to turn away from it. Reproof, when done in love and humility, can lead to transformation and restoration.

2. Rebuke: Sometimes, we encounter situations where a strong and direct correction is necessary. Rebuking involves firmly and boldly addressing falsehoods or ungodly behavior. It requires courage and discernment, ensuring that our words are guided by God's truth and motivated by love, with the aim of restoring individuals to a right relationship with God.

3. Exhort: The Word of God is also meant to encourage, uplift, and inspire. It offers hope, comfort, and guidance in times of trial and difficulty. As we share God's Word, we should seek to exhort others, reminding them of God's promises, His faithfulness, and the abundant life found in Christ.

It is crucial to remember that our approach should be characterized by "complete patience and teaching." We should be patient with those who may not immediately accept or understand the message. Patience allows room for the Holy Spirit to work in hearts and minds, bringing about conviction and transformation in His perfect timing. Additionally, we should present the Word of God with sound teaching, ensuring accuracy and clarity in our communication.

Let's reflect on our readiness to share God's Word. Are we actively studying and growing in our knowledge of Scripture? Are we willing to reprove, rebuke, and exhort, guided by love and humility? Let's purpose to be like Timothy, faithful messengers of the truth, ready to proclaim God's Word in season and out of season. May our lives and words be a testament to the transformative power of God's Word, drawing others closer to Him.

Prayer: Father, in Jesus' name, I thank You for the precious gift of Your Word. Help me to be diligent in studying and understanding it so that I may be ready to share it with others. Give me wisdom, love, and patience as I share Your word with those around me. I declare Your word will penetrate my heart and transform lives for Your glory. In Jesus' name, I pray. Amen.

CHAPTER 2

Be Watchful

"Be watchful, stand firm in the faith, and be strong."
1 Corinthians 16:13 (ESV)

As **Defenders of the Faith,** we must be watchful at all times, like a good soldier in the middle of a war.

We live in a world that constantly bombards us with distractions, temptations, and challenges. The apostle Paul's words to the Corinthians carry a timeless message: "Be watchful." These two words are a call to alertness and spiritual vigilance, urging believers to remain steadfast in their faith, resolute in their actions, and strong in their convictions. Let's explore the significance of being watchful and how it can transform our lives.

To be watchful means to be awake and attentive, guarding against potential dangers, both seen and unseen. As Christ followers, we are called to be watchful not only of external circumstances but also of the spiritual realm. The enemy seeks to deceive, distract, and derail us from our faith. So, it is essential that we remain vigilant, discerning the signs of spiritual warfare and guarding our hearts against the attacks of the evil one.

You see watchfulness requires a conscious effort to stay connected to God through prayer, His Word, and fellowship with other believers. These spiritual disciplines strengthen our discernment, enabling us to recognize the schemes of the enemy and resist his temptations. By cultivating an intimate relationship with God, we gain wisdom, clarity, and a heightened sense of spiritual awareness.

Being watchful means standing firm in the faith. The world may challenge our beliefs, trying to mold us according to its values. However, when we remain rooted in God's truth, our faith becomes unshakable. We must hold fast to the teachings of Scripture, refusing to compromise our convictions or water down the Gospel message. Our unwavering faith becomes a testimony of God's faithfulness and the hope He provides in a world longing for truth.

In addition, being watchful compels us to be strong. This phrase urges us to exercise courage and boldness, in our faith journey. It means taking a stand for righteousness, pursuing holiness, and living out our calling with determination and conviction. It's in our strength in Christ that we find the ability to resist the pressures of the world, overcome temptations, and persevere in the face of adversity.

As we are watchful, we become more sensitive to the leading of the Holy Spirit. We develop a heightened sensitivity to His promptings, which guide us in the paths of righteousness and direct our steps. The Holy Spirit empowers us to discern between good and evil, truth and deception, enabling us to make wise choices that align with God's will.

The call to be watchful carries great significance in our Christian walk. It's a reminder to remain alert, vigilant, and spiritually attuned in a world that often seeks to distract and deceive us. By standing firm in our faith, acting with courage, and relying on God's strength, we can navigate the challenges and temptations that come our way. Let's commit ourselves to a life of watchfulness, seeking God's guidance, and relying on His power to sustain us.

Prayer: Father, in the name of Jesus, I purpose in my heart to be watchful and vigilant. I will be strong and take a stand for righteousness. I will allow the Holy Spirit to lead me in the direction I am to go and will depend on Him in all things. In Jesus' name, I pray. Amen.

CHAPTER 3

Becoming an Imitator of God

"Therefore, be imitators of God, as beloved children."
Ephesians 5:1 (ESV)

As **Defenders of the Faith,** we are called to be imitators of Christ. Jesus said He only did what He saw the Father do and only said what He heard the Father say. We are to be imitators of Christ and develop that type of relationship with the Father, Jesus, and the Holy Spirit.

In the book of Ephesians, the apostle Paul presents a powerful exhortation to the believers in Ephesus. He encourages them to live a life that reflects the very nature of God. Among the many instructions, he emphasizes the importance of becoming imitators of God. This call to imitation is not a suggestion but a divine invitation to participate in God's character and embody His love in our daily lives.

You see, to be an imitator of God is to live in a way that imitates His nature, His love, and His righteousness. It's a call to reflect His goodness and holiness, imitating His actions, attitudes, and intentions. As Christ followers, we are called to reflect God's love and demonstrate it in all our relationships.

I think about my kids, especially my two sons, who, when people see them, say, "Oh, they look just like you. They are a mirror image of you. His mannerisms are like yours." Why is that? Because he spends a lot of time around me. He has the same DNA as I do. We have a close relationship. This is what God desires us to experience with Him. You see, God has designed you to experience a relationship with Him like a child with a father. He loves us because we are His children, and He's created us for a relationship with Him that leads to imitation. People should say you love just like God does and act just like He does.

First and foremost, we are reminded that we are beloved children of God. Our imitation of Him is not out of obligation or duty but flows from a deep understanding of His love for us. It's in this place of love that we find the motivation and strength to live as imitators of God. As we embrace our identity as God's children, we will reflect His love, which our world desperately needs.

19

Imitating God requires intentional effort. It involves examining our hearts, minds, and actions to ensure that they align with His will. It means surrendering our selfish desires and embracing selflessness. In a culture that promotes self-centeredness, being an imitator of God is a countercultural stance that can transform lives and impact eternity.

One of the primary ways we imitate God is through love. God's love is unconditional, sacrificial, and forgiving. It goes beyond the boundaries of human understanding. As imitators of God, we are called to love others in the same way. We are called to extend grace, forgiveness, and compassion even to those who may not deserve it. Through our love, we have the opportunity to reveal God's heart to a broken world.

Being an imitator of God is not an individual effort. It's a collective pursuit that involves the body of Christ, the Church. As believers, we are called to encourage and support one another in this journey of imitation. We can learn from one another, hold each other accountable, and spur one another on toward greater Christlikeness.

In our pursuit of imitating God, we must also remember that it is a lifelong process. We will make mistakes, stumble, and fall. But in those moments, we can seek God's forgiveness, extend it to others, and continue striving to reflect His love. God's grace is sufficient, and His Spirit empowers us to press on in our imitation of Him.

So, today, let's respond to Paul's exhortation with renewed commitment. Let's embrace our identity as beloved children of God and begin the journey of becoming imitators of our Heavenly Father. Allow His love to be the driving force behind your actions, attitudes, and relationships. As we imitate Him, our lives will be a testimony to His transformative power and a source of hope in a world in need of genuine love.

Prayer: Father, in Jesus' name, I thank You for calling me to imitate You as a beloved child. Help me to live in a way that reflects Your love and righteousness. Empower me by Your Spirit to love others unconditionally, sacrificially, and selflessly. I know that my imitation of You will bring glory to Your name and draw others into a relationship with You. In Jesus' name, I pray. Amen.

CHAPTER 4

Being Rooted

Rooted and built up in him and established in the faith, just as you were taught, abounding in thanksgiving."
Colossians 2:7 (ESV)

As **Defenders of the Faith,** in order to fulfill the will of God in our lives, we must be rooted, grounded, and built up in him and established in the faith.

In the hustle and bustle of our lives, we find ourselves seeking stability, searching for something unshakeable that can anchor us in the middle of the storms of life. The world offers numerous sources of security and fulfillment, but they all prove to be temporary. As Christ followers, we are called to a different path—a path that leads us to be rooted and established in Christ.

Colossians 2:7 provides us with a powerful image of what it means to be rooted in Christ. Just as a tree draws its strength and nourishment from its roots, we are called to draw our strength from our deep connection with Jesus. Being rooted in Christ means that our faith is firmly established in Him, allowing us to withstand the challenges and trials that come our way.

To be rooted in Christ, we must first recognize the source of our spiritual nourishment. Just as a tree's roots dig deep into the ground to access water and nutrients, we need to dig deep into God's Word and His presence through prayer. The Bible is our spiritual food, providing us with wisdom, guidance, and encouragement. As we study and meditate on the Word of God, our roots grow deeper, enabling us to stand firm in our faith.

Additionally, being rooted in Christ requires us to be firmly established in the faith. We must have a solid foundation of understanding and belief in the core teachings of Christianity. This foundation is built through sound teaching, discipleship, and fellowship with other believers. As we grow in our knowledge of God's truth, our roots grow stronger, anchoring us in the unchanging power of the gospel.

Being rooted in Christ also means embracing a lifestyle of gratitude. The verse in Colossians tells us that as we are rooted and built up in Him, we should abound in thanksgiving. Gratitude is a natural outpouring of a heart that is deeply rooted in Christ. When we recognize the depth of God's love and the abundance of His blessings, our hearts overflow with thankfulness. Gratitude not only nourishes our own souls but also inspires and encourages others around us.

When we are rooted in Christ, our lives bear fruit. Just as a healthy tree produces abundant fruit, a life deeply connected to Christ overflows with the fruit of the Spirit: love, joy, peace, patience, kindness, goodness, faithfulness, gentleness, and self-control (Galatians 5:22–23). These qualities not only bless us personally but also impact those around us, drawing them closer to the source of our strength.

Today, let's reflect on our own spiritual roots. Are we deeply connected to Christ? Are we drawing nourishment from His Word and His presence? Are we firmly established in the faith with a solid foundation of biblical knowledge and belief? And are we abounding in thanksgiving, recognizing, and appreciating the countless blessings God has bestowed upon us?

As we answer these questions and seek to deepen our roots in Christ, let's remember that being rooted is a lifelong process. It requires intentional effort, consistent devotion, and a desire to continually grow in our relationship with Him. Let's decide to be like trees firmly planted by streams of water, continually nourished by the living water of Christ, and bearing fruit that brings glory to God.

Prayer: Father, in the name of Jesus, I thank You for the gift of being rooted in Christ. Help me to continually draw my strength and nourishment from Him and may my life bear abundant fruit for Your glory. Guide me as I deepen my roots through studying Your word, prayer, and fellowship with other believers. May gratitude overflow from my heart, impacting those around me and drawing them closer to You. In Jesus' name, I pray. Amen.

CHAPTER 5

Believing in Signs and Wonders

"And these signs will accompany those who believe in my name, they will cast out demons; they will speak in new tongues; they will pick up serpents with their hands; if they drink any deadly poison, it will not hurt them; they will lay their hands on the sick, and they will recover."
Mark 16:17-18 (ESV)

As **Defenders of the Faith**, God will call us into dark places where people are demon-possessed, sick, and hopeless. We must be prepared to pray for them; casting out devils, healing the sick, and seeing people restored.

The closing words of the Gospel of Mark contain a powerful promise and a challenge to every believer. Jesus declares that those who believe in Him will experience signs and wonders as they walk in obedience to His name. These signs include casting out demons, speaking in new tongues, handling dangerous snakes unharmed, and having the ability to withstand deadly poisons. In addition, believers will have the power to lay hands on the sick, and they will be healed.

At first glance, these verses may seem unbelievable. We may question whether such extraordinary acts of faith are still relevant today. However, the fundamental message in these words transcends time and remains as relevant as ever. Jesus is reminding us that faith in Him empowers us to overcome the challenges we face and to accomplish things that surpass our human limitations.

Believing in Jesus means placing our complete trust and reliance on Him. It is a confident assurance that He is who He claims to be—the Son of God, our Savior, and the source of our strength. When we fully surrender our lives to Him, we enter into a relationship that surpasses our natural abilities and enables us to live in the supernatural power of God.

Jesus promises that signs and wonders will accompany those who believe. These signs are not mere manifestations of power but serve a greater purpose—to validate the truth of the Gospel and draw people to faith. Through miracles, God reveals Himself to the world and demonstrates His compassion, love, and desire for all people to experience His grace.

Believing in Jesus is not limited to a mental acknowledgment or a casual association. It is an active, living faith that produces visible evidence. As we submit ourselves to Christ and walk in obedience to His teachings, we position ourselves to experience the miraculous and witness God's power at work in and through us.

However, it's crucial to understand that the signs and wonders mentioned in these verses are not the ultimate goal. They are means to an end—to bring glory to God, to demonstrate His love, and to advance His kingdom. They are expressions of God's power and grace, but they should never overshadow the message of salvation and the transformation of hearts.

Today, as Christ followers, we are called to embrace the promises of God's Word and walk in faith. We are invited to step out of our comfort zones, pray boldly, trust God for the impossible, and expect His supernatural intervention in our lives and the lives of others. It is not a call to seek personal glory or to boast about our abilities, but rather to be vessels through which God's power can flow to touch the lives of those around us.

Let's remember that the signs and wonders Jesus mentioned are not limited to a select few. They are available to every believer who earnestly seeks the Lord, abides in His Word, and walks in obedience. Our faith, though it may start as a mustard seed, has the potential to move mountains, transform lives, and reveal God's glory to the world.

Prayer: Father, in Jesus' name, I thank You for the promise of signs and wonders that accompany those who believe in Jesus. Help me to cultivate a faith that is unwavering and rooted in Your word. Strengthen my trust in You so that I may step out in obedience and experience Your supernatural power in my life. My life will be a testament to Your love and grace, drawing others to a saving knowledge of Jesus Christ. In Jesus' name, I pray. Amen.

CHAPTER 6

Chosen by God

"But you are a chosen race, a royal priesthood, a holy nation, a people for his own possession, that you may proclaim the excellencies of him who called you out of darkness into his marvelous light."
1 Peter 2:9 (ESV)

As **Defenders of the Faith,** we have been chosen by God. In other words, He handpicked you and me. The adversary may seem powerful, dangerous, and dominant. But look again. You are God's chosen: "a people for his own possession."

I Remember playing basketball as a kid in elementary school and dividing up the teams. Usually, the two best players would be captains, and as they were choosing sides, you were thinking, I hope I get chosen by this team because they are the winning team. If you were chosen by that team—remember how great it felt to be chosen by the best player? On the other hand, remember how bad you felt when they got down to the last two or three and you still were not chosen?

When you are chosen and accepted, it raises your self-esteem. How awesome is it to know that God personally chose and valued you? His purpose is for you to help build the kingdom of God.

In the book of 1 Peter, we find a powerful message for believers, reminding us of our divine identity in Christ. We are God's chosen people. The apostle Peter writes to the early Christians, revealing a powerful truth that can change our lives and give us the strength to overcome anything a fallen world throws at us.

The word "chosen" carries great significance. It implies being specially selected, set apart, and called for a specific purpose. When we accept Jesus Christ as our Lord and Savior, we become part of a chosen race. Our identity is no longer determined by worldly standards. Instead, we are set apart as children of the King.

Not only are we a chosen race, but we are also called a royal priesthood. In ancient times, priests held a significant role as intermediaries between God and humanity, offering sacrifices and interceding on behalf of others. In Christ, we have direct access to God's presence, and we are commissioned to be spiritual priests in this world. We have the privilege of representing God's love, extending His grace, and interceding for those who are lost and in need of salvation.

Additionally, we are called a holy nation. We are set apart to live a life that reflects God's holiness and righteousness. Our words, actions, and attitudes should align with the character of Christ. As ambassadors of the Kingdom, we carry the responsibility to bring light into darkness, hope into despair, and love into a broken world. We are called to stand firm in our convictions, even when faced with opposition, and shine with God's truth and grace.

We are identified as a people for God's own possession. We are treasured by the Creator of the universe. The fact that we are beloved children of God determines our worth and value rather than our accomplishments or the opinions of others. We are purchased with the precious blood of Jesus Christ, and we belong to Him completely. Our identity is found in God's possession, and this truth brings security, significance, and purpose to our lives.

As we embrace our divine identity as the chosen ones, let's also remember our purpose: to proclaim the excellencies of Him who called us out of darkness into His marvelous light. We are called to be witnesses of God's love, grace, and power. Our lives should be a testimony to the transformative work of Christ within us. We have the incredible privilege of sharing the Good News and pointing others toward the hope found in Jesus Christ.

Let's live today with the knowledge that God has chosen us, given us His Spirit to equip us, and given us a mission bigger than ourselves. May our lives reflect the beauty of our divine identity as we walk in the light, love, and grace of our Savior, Jesus Christ.

Prayer: Father, in Jesus' name, I thank You for choosing me and calling me into a personal relationship with You. Help me to fully embrace my divine identity as Your child and empower me to live a life that reflects Your glory. Use me as an instrument of Your love and grace to touch the lives of those around me. In Jesus' name, I pray. Amen.

CHAPTER 7

Confidence that is Unshakable in Christ

"In him and through faith in him, we may approach God with freedom and confidence."
Ephesians 3:12 (NIV)

As **Defenders of the Faith,** we have complete access to God, which is one of the greatest privileges given to humankind. This means we are able to approach Him with confidence.

Confidence is a valuable characteristic that helps us navigate through life's challenges with strength. It empowers us to step out of our comfort zone, pursue our dreams, and overcome obstacles that come our way. However, worldly confidence often stems from our own abilities, achievements, or the approval of others. The Bible, on the other hand, encourages us to find our unwavering confidence in Christ alone.

Have you ever heard someone pray with boldness and confidence and thought, to yourself, "I wish I could pray with that same boldness and confidence." The good news is we can have that same boldness and confidence because of our faith in Jesus Christ.

In Ephesians 3:12, the Apostle Paul reminds us that our confidence is rooted in our relationship with Jesus. He writes, "In him and through faith in him, we may approach God with freedom and confidence." This verse beautifully describes the essence of our faith and the assurance we have as believers.

Our confidence begins with the realization that we are in Christ. Through faith in Him, we have been united with Him in a profound and transformative way. We are no longer constrained by our past failures or our own shortcomings. In Christ, we find forgiveness, redemption, and a new identity as children of God. This truth should ignite within us an unshakable confidence that transcends circumstances and defies human logic.

The foundation of our confidence in Christ lies in His perfect work on the cross. It is through His sacrifice that we have access to God and can approach Him freely. We no longer need to fear condemnation or feel unworthy of His presence.

Jesus has opened the way for us to boldly come before the throne of grace, knowing that we are loved, accepted, and welcomed as His beloved children.

This freedom to approach God with confidence should transform the way we live our lives. When we truly understand the depth of God's love for us and the access we have to His presence, it changes everything. We no longer need to rely on our own strength or the approval of others to feel secure. Our confidence is firmly rooted in the unchanging character of God.

In a world that constantly bombards us with messages of self-doubt, comparison, and the pursuit of perfection, we can find comfort and strength in our identity as children of God. Our confidence is not based on our own abilities or achievements but on the unending grace and love of our Heavenly Father.

When we live in the fullness of this confidence, we become bold witnesses of God's goodness and grace to those around us. The ups and downs of life do not easily shake the trust that is evident in our lives. We become vessels through which

God's power and love can flow, making a lasting impact on the lives of others.

So, today, let's embrace the truth of Ephesians 3:12 and find our unshakable confidence in Christ. Let's approach each day with the assurance that comes from knowing and accepting our Heavenly Father's love. As we walk in the confidence of our identity in Him, our lives will reflect the transformative power of the Gospel, drawing others to experience the same hope, freedom, and confidence in Jesus Christ.

Prayer: Father, in Jesus' name, I thank You for the unshakable confidence I have in You. Help me to daily embrace my identity as Your child and find my worth and security in You alone. Fill me with Your Holy Spirit and empower me to live a life that reflects the confidence I have in Christ. May my words and actions draw others to experience the same freedom and assurance found in a relationship with You. In Jesus' name, I pray, Amen.

CHAPTER 8

Continue in What You Have Been Taught

But as for you, continue in what you have learned and have become convinced of, because you know those from whom you learned it.

2 Timothy 3:14 (NIV)

As **Defenders of the Faith,** we must continue in the things we have learned, not just for ourselves but for others. We will finish the good work that God has started in each of our lives and enable Him to use us for His honor and glory as we submit to His leading and guidance.

As a sports fan, I have watched many games, especially basketball games, where my team, the Lakers, would have a large lead and all of a sudden go from playing to win to playing not to lose because they got comfortable with a big lead, and slowly but surely that lead began to dwindle, even to the point of losing that game, which at one point seemed impossible to happen.

That is what Paul is encouraging Timothy to avoid. "You've started off well," Paul says; "don't change that. Continue doing what you're doing." And what are the things Timothy has learned? Paul says, "From infancy, you have known the Holy Scriptures, which are able to make you wise for salvation through faith in Christ Jesus. All Scripture is God-breathed and is useful for teaching, for rebuking, for correcting, and for training in righteousness, so that the men and women of God may be complete and well equipped for every good work."

Anything new can seem very appealing. But as the apostle Paul cautioned his young protégé Timothy, our beliefs and teaching must always be founded on the timeless truth of the Gospel of Jesus Christ.

The reminder Paul gave to Timothy is equally vital for Christians today, as we are pounded on every side by twisted teachings, false doctrine, a sacrilegious 'spirituality' that has slithered into the Church today, and a compromised, watered-down gospel that is causing many to stumble in their Christian walk.

Not only are we to hear the truth, but we are to know the Word of God intimately. We are to come to a personal assurance that God's Word is true, and His promises never fail. We must remember that nothing is more important in this God-hating, Christ-rejecting, sinful world than to walk in the light of the glorious gospel of Jesus Christ and KNOW in whom we have believed.

Prayer: Father, in the name of Jesus, I thank You for Your word, which stands eternal. I will continue to do the things I have been taught and will finish the good work that You began in me. In Jesus' name, I pray. Amen.

CHAPTER 9

Courage to be Bold

*"But though we had already suffered and been shamefully
treated at Philippi, as you know, we had boldness
in our God to declare to you the gospel of God in
the midst of much conflict."*
1 Thessalonians 2:2 (NLT)

As **Defenders of the Faith,** we all want our lives to count; we want to make a difference in this world. It was Paul's boldness in evangelizing that kept his life from being in vain.

In our journey of faith, we often encounter challenges and opposition that test our resolve and courage. The apostle Paul, in his letter to the Thessalonian believers, shares a powerful testimony of courage in the face of adversity. He recounts the trials and mistreatment he and his companions endured in Philippi, yet despite the hardships, they remained steadfast in their mission to proclaim the gospel. It is through this example that we learn about the transformative power of courage in our own lives.

Courage is not the absence of fear but rather the ability to press forward despite it. Paul and his companions faced physical suffering and shame, but their faith in God provided them with the boldness to continue sharing the good news. Their courage did not come from their own strength or resilience but from their unwavering trust in God's provision and protection.

We are not exempt from the conflicts and challenges the world throws at us. We may face opposition from different sources— whether it be the pressures of society, personal struggles, or even persecution for our faith. However, as Christ followers, we are called to respond with courage, just as Paul and his companions did.

Courage is born from a deep-rooted relationship with God. It is nurtured through prayer, the study of His Word, and the fellowship of believers. When we cultivate an intimate connection with our Heavenly Father, we discover that our strength is not limited to our own abilities but is found in His power. As we draw near to Him, He infuses us with the courage needed to face any trial that comes our way.

Courage is contagious. Paul's boldness in the midst of conflict inspired and encouraged the Thessalonian believers. When we walk in courage, we become living testimonies of God's faithfulness and provision. Our unwavering commitment to the truth of the gospel influences those around us, enabling them to find the strength to persevere through their own trials.

Courage allows us to move beyond the limits of our comfort zones and step into God's divine plan for our lives. It empowers us to overcome obstacles, push through adversity, and embrace opportunities for growth. When we surrender our fears and trust in God's guidance, we are on a journey that leads to transformation and spiritual maturity.

Let's not let the difficulties and conflicts we face demotivate us. Instead, let's draw strength from Paul and his companions' example. Let's remember that our God is greater than any challenge we face, and He equips us with the courage we need to stand firm in our faith. May our lives be a living testament to the transformative power of courage—declaring the gospel boldly and loving others fearlessly, even in the midst of adversity.

Prayer: Father, in Jesus' name, I thank You for the example of courage I find in the lives of Paul and his companions. Empower me by Your Spirit to face my trials with boldness and unwavering faith. Help me to trust in Your provision and guidance, knowing that You are always with me. My life be a testimony of Your love and faithfulness. In Jesus' name, I pray. Amen.

CHAPTER 10

Defending the Faith

"Dear friends, I had been eagerly planning to write to you about the salvation we all share. But now I find that I must write about something else, urging you to defend the faith that God has entrusted once for all time to his holy people."

Jude 1:3 (NLT)

As **Defenders of the Faith,** we are called to embrace God's Word and never waver in defending the truth of the Gospel.

In the book of Jude, we find a heartfelt appeal from the brother of James, urging fellow believers to defend the faith that has been entrusted to them. Although Jude initially intended to write about the wonderful salvation they shared, a pressing need arose to address the critical matter of preserving and protecting the truth of the Gospel. This timeless message is just as relevant to us today as it was to the early Christians.

As Christ followers, we are called to embrace and proclaim the truth of God's Word. However, we live in a world where the values and beliefs of society are continually shifting, making it increasingly challenging to stand firm in our faith. The enemy seeks to distort and discredit the Gospel, sowing seeds of doubt and confusion. That is why Jude's exhortation to defend the faith holds profound significance for us.

To defend the faith is to actively engage in the spiritual battle for truth. It involves both an inward conviction and an outward expression. We must first anchor ourselves in the unchanging truth of God's Word, immersing ourselves in it and allowing it to shape our beliefs and worldview. A strong foundation in the Word equips us to discern falsehood and counter the attacks on our faith.

Furthermore, defending the faith requires courage and perseverance. It means being prepared to offer a loving defense when our beliefs are challenged. We must remember that our battle is not against flesh and blood but against the spiritual forces of darkness (Ephesians 6:12). Therefore, even when facing opposition, our response should always be one of love, humility, and gentleness.

Defending the faith also involves leading lives that reflect the transforming power of the Gospel. Our actions and attitudes should be consistent with the truth we profess. The world is watching, and our lives are a living testimony of the hope and truth we hold. As we exemplify Christ's love and character, we become powerful witnesses, drawing others to the faith we defend.

In our defense of the faith, we must also remember that it is ultimately God's truth we are upholding. We do not defend our faith in our own strength or wisdom but rely on the guidance of the Holy Spirit. We must fervently seek the Lord's leading, trusting that He will equip us with the necessary wisdom and discernment to effectively defend the truth.

Finally, let's take heart from the knowledge that the faith we uphold is not flimsy or vulnerable. It's a faith that has been entrusted "once for all time" to God's holy people (Jude 1:3). The Gospel message remains unchanging, and its power to transform lives is as potent today as it was in the early days of the Church. God's truth stands firm and immovable in the middle of the shifting sands of culture and human opinion.

As we navigate the challenges of our time, may we take Jude's call to defend the faith to heart. Let's steadfastly hold to the truth of God's Word while actively participating in the spiritual conflict for truth and following the Holy Spirit's leading. In doing so, we can confidently face the challenges that come our way, secure in the knowledge that our faith is anchored in the unshakable foundation of God's eternal truth.

Prayer: Father, in Jesus' name, I thank You for the precious gift of faith. Help me to be a faithful steward of this truth and actively defend it with love, humility, and wisdom. Fill me with Your Holy Spirit so that I may discern and counter the attacks on my faith. Give me the strength and courage to stand firm in the face of opposition, and may my life be a living testimony of the hope I have in You. In Jesus' name, I pray. Amen.

CHAPTER 11

Destroying Arguments

"We destroy arguments and every lofty opinion raised
against the knowledge of God and take every
thought captive to obey Christ."
2 Corinthians 10:5 (ESV)

As **Defenders of the Faith,** we find ourselves constantly in a War. Where is this war fought? The war is fought in our thought life.

In our journey of faith, we often find ourselves facing various arguments and opposing opinions that challenge our beliefs and knowledge of God. These arguments can come from the world, our own doubts, or even from the enemy himself. However, as followers of Christ, we are called to stand firm and actively engage in the spiritual battle for truth and righteousness.

The Apostle Paul, in his second letter to the Corinthians, reminds us of the importance of destroying arguments and taking captive every thought that goes against the knowledge of God. But how can we effectively accomplish this? Let's look at a few key principles found in Scripture.

1. Know the Truth: Jesus said, "I am the way, and the truth, and the life" (John 14:6). To effectively destroy arguments, we must first be grounded in the truth of God's Word. Spend time daily studying and meditating on the Scriptures, allowing the Holy Spirit to reveal the truth to you. The more we know and understand God's truth, the better equipped we are to discern and refute false arguments.

2. Put on the Armor of God: Ephesians 6:11–17 teaches us about the armor of God, which equips us for spiritual battle. Each piece of the armor, such as the belt of truth, the breastplate of righteousness, and the sword of the Spirit, helps us stand firm against arguments and falsehoods. Dress yourself in this spiritual armor daily, seeking God's protection and strength as you engage in the battle.

3. Renew Your Mind: Romans 12:2 urges us not to conform to the patterns of this world but to be transformed by the renewing of our minds. Fill your mind with positive and uplifting thoughts by focusing

on what is true, noble, right, pure, lovely, admirable, excellent, and praiseworthy (Philippians 4:8). When our minds are renewed by God's truth, we can discern and reject arguments that contradict His Word.

Prayer: Father, in the name of Jesus, equip me with your truth and help me discern and destroy arguments that oppose your knowledge. Renew my mind and give me the wisdom to stand firm in love. I will take every thought captive to obey Christ. In Jesus' name, I pray. Amen.

CHAPTER 12

Embracing God's Authority with Humility

"Jesus called his twelve disciples together and gave them authority to cast out evil spirits and to heal every kind of disease and illness."
Matthew 10:1 (NLT)

As **Defenders of the Faith,** we must consider the authority that Jesus empowered us with in order to preach the gospel and see people saved, healed, delivered, and set free.

In Matthew 10:1, we witness a significant moment when Jesus gave authority to His twelve disciples. This act of empowerment was not a symbolic gesture but a transformative experience that would shape their lives and the course of history. As Christ followers today, we can draw invaluable lessons from this passage and understand how we too can embrace and exercise God's authority in our lives.

First and foremost, it is crucial to acknowledge the source of all authority. Jesus, being the Son of God, possessed absolute authority over all things. As Christ followers, our authority stems from our relationship with Him. We do not hold power in and of ourselves but are called to operate under the delegated authority of our Lord and Savior. This truth should keep us grounded in humility and foster a deep sense of dependence on God.

The authority given to the disciples was not given for personal gain or to boast about their own abilities. Rather, it was a divine commission to serve and minister to others. Jesus granted them the authority to cast out evil spirits and heal the sick, enabling them to bring hope and restoration to those in need. As modern-day disciples, we are called to use the authority entrusted to us for the betterment of others and the advancement of God's Kingdom.

The disciples' authority was not without its challenges. In the following verses of Matthew 10, Jesus warned them of the opposition they would face. They were to expect persecution, rejection, and even betrayal. However, they were also promised that God's Spirit would guide and empower them in their journey. This reminds us that as we step into our God-given authority, we will encounter trials and opposition, but we can find strength and courage in the Holy Spirit who dwells within us.

As recipients of God's authority, we must exercise it with wisdom and discernment. Just as Jesus taught the disciples, we are called to be shrewd as serpents and innocent as doves (Matthew 10:16). Our authority should be exercised in accordance with God's Word, aligning our actions with His will and reflecting His character. It is a responsibility that requires humility, prayer, and an unwavering commitment to seek God's guidance in all our endeavors.

Finally, love and compassion should always go hand in hand with the authority we, as Christ followers, possess. Jesus, throughout His ministry, demonstrated the power of love in His acts of healing and deliverance. Our authority should be exercised in a way that reflects Christ's love and extends His grace to those we encounter. By showing kindness, empathy, and a willingness to serve, we can effectively demonstrate the transformative power of God's authority in our lives.

Through our relationship with Christ, we have been given the privilege and responsibility to represent Him in this world. May we embrace this authority with humility, relying on the Holy Spirit's guidance, exercising it with wisdom and love, and ultimately bringing glory to our heavenly Father.

Prayer: Father, in Jesus' name, I thank You for entrusting me with the authority to represent You in this world. Help me to walk in humility, recognizing that my authority comes from You alone. Guide me in using this authority to serve and bless others, always seeking Your wisdom and direction. Fill me with Your Holy Spirit, that I may operate in the power and love of Christ. In Jesus' name, I pray. Amen.

CHAPTER 13

Embracing the Power Within

"For God has not given us a spirit of fear but of power, of love, and of a sound mind."
2 Timothy 1:7 (NKJV)

As **Defenders of the Faith,** we must not be silent or timid with our testimonies of how Christ changed and transformed our lives.

In a world filled with uncertainty and challenges, fear seems to hide at every corner, seeking to cripple our faith and hinder our progress. Yet, as Christ followers, we have been given a precious gift—a spirit of power, love, and a sound mind. These divine attributes enable us to navigate through life's trials with unwavering confidence and unyielding faith. Today, let's delve into the depths of this powerful truth and uncover the transformative impact it can have on our lives.

First, we are assured that God has not given us a spirit of fear. Fear can paralyze us, robbing us of the joy, peace, and purpose

God intends for us to experience. It limits our potential and hinders our progress. However, as children of God, we can take comfort in knowing that fear does not originate from Him. Instead, He has equipped us with a spirit of power. This power is not a worldly force; the divine strength that flows through us is the Holy Spirit. He enables us to overcome obstacles, conquer challenges, and walk in victory, even in the face of adversity.

Second, this verse reminds us that God has given us a spirit of love. In a world that often promotes hatred, division, and animosity, the power of love can be a remarkable testimony of God's transformative work in our lives. It empowers us to extend grace, forgiveness, and compassion toward others, even when it seems impossible. Love compels us to act selflessly, seeking the well-being of others above our own. It breaks down barriers, brings healing to broken relationships, and offers hope to the hurting. Let's embrace this spirit of love and allow it to permeate every aspect of our lives.

And finally, we are given the spirit of a sound mind. In a culture marked by confusion, anxiety, and overwhelming distractions, having a sound mind is a precious gift. It enables us to think clearly, make wise decisions, and discern the voice of God in the middle of the noise of the world. A sound mind is not one filled with worry or doubt but rather one anchored in the truth of God's Word. It allows us to focus on the things that are good, pure, and praiseworthy, enabling us to live a life that brings honor and glory to our Heavenly Father.

As we reflect on 2 Timothy 1:7, let's remember that the power, love, and sound mind we possess are not products of our own strength or abilities. They are gifts bestowed upon us by our loving Heavenly Father. We need to lean on Him and rely on His power to work through us. We should seek His guidance and direction in every aspect of our lives. When we surrender our fears, our worries, and our limitations to Him, we tap into a reservoir of strength and potential that transcends human understanding.

Let's rely on God's strength, trusting that He who has called us is faithful to equip us for every task. May our lives be a testimony to the incredible power of our God, drawing others to Him and bringing glory to His name.

Prayer: Father, in Jesus' name, I thank You for the spirit of power, love, and a sound mind that You have given me. Help me to fully embrace these divine attributes and to walk in the confidence of who I am in Christ. Strengthen me when fear arises, empower me to love as You love, and give me a sound mind to discern Your will in all circumstances. May Your power work mightily in me, enabling me to live out my faith victoriously and bring glory to Your name. In Jesus' name, I pray, Amen.

CHAPTER 14

God Delivers from Trials to Triumph

"Many are the afflictions of the righteous, but the
Lord delivers him out of them all."
Psalms 34:19 (ESV)

As **Defenders of the Faith,** we understand that trust in God is foundational in our relationship with Him and is the key to living in His delivering power.

As you know, life is a journey filled with ups and downs, joys and sorrows. As Christ followers, we are not immune to the trials and tribulations that come our way. However, we do have a promise from God that He will deliver us from every affliction we face. In Psalms 34:19, we are reminded that "Many are the afflictions of the righteous, but the Lord delivers him out of them all." This verse assures us that even in our darkest moments, God is working on our behalf, ready to bring us out of every difficult situation. Good news, wouldn't you say?

Now, it's crucial to understand that being a righteous person does not mean we will not have challenges. In fact, the Bible tells us that we will face trials of various kinds (James 1:2). We may encounter health issues, financial struggles, broken relationships, or overwhelming circumstances that seem impossible to overcome. Yet, in the midst of our afflictions, we can find comfort in the promise of our heavenly Father to deliver us.

God's deliverance is not limited to a specific type of affliction or a particular duration of suffering. His deliverance is comprehensive and all-encompassing. He is the God who parted the Red Sea, healed the sick, and raised the dead. He is the same God who can bring healing to our bodies, restore our broken hearts, and lift us out of the deepest pits of despair. No matter what we are facing, we can trust in His faithfulness and His power to deliver us.

Always remember that it's essential to understand that God's deliverance may not always come in the way we expect or in the timeframe we desire. Sometimes, He allows us to walk through the fire to refine our character and strengthen our faith. Other times, He may choose to deliver us instantly, displaying His miraculous power on the spot. Regardless of His method, we can be confident that God is working all things together for our good (Romans 8:28).

While we wait for God's deliverance, we will find comfort and strength by seeking His presence and relying on His promises. You'll find the Bible is filled with many stories of God's faithfulness and His miraculous work in the lives of His people. By meditating on these stories and testimonies, we can build our faith and trust that if God delivered them, He will deliver us as well. Amen?

In times of challenge, we are called to hold on to God and pour out our hearts before Him in prayer. He is not distant or indifferent to our pain; He is a compassionate Father who stands ready to comfort and rescue His children. As we cast our burdens upon Him and surrender our anxieties, we open the door for His deliverance to manifest in our lives.

Let's be confident today, knowing that the challenges we face are temporary. Thank God for that! We serve a God who is mighty to save and deliver. He is with us in every trial, and

His deliverance is sure. As we walk through the valley of the shadow of death, we fear no evil, for He is with us (Psalm 23:4). Our deliverance is on the horizon, and through it, we will emerge stronger, wiser, and more steadfast in our faith.

Prayer: Father, in Jesus' name, I thank You for Your promise of deliverance. Help me to trust in Your faithfulness even in the midst of afflictions. Strengthen my faith and give me the patience to wait for Your perfect timing. I surrender my burdens to You and invite Your presence to bring healing and deliverance into my life. May Your name be glorified through every trial I face. In Jesus' name, I pray. Amen.

CHAPTER 15

God Trains My Hands for War

*Praise the Lord, who is my rock. He **trains** my hands for war and gives my fingers skills for battle.*
Psalms 144:1 (NLT)

As **Defenders of the Faith,** we must realize that Life isn't a playground but a battleground. You may not know why you're in a battle, but you can be sure God wants to teach you something. He's walking you through an exercise in learning.

From the bears and lions of his youth to the Philistine champion Goliath and leading armies into battle, God enabled David to fight and win those battles. And although our battles may be different, the same God that helped and trained David's hands for war is the same God that is helping and training our hands for whatever battles come our way.

In Hebrew, the word trains from Psalm 144 is also translated as teaches, and it means to goad. A goad is a sharp stick that is used to make animals move forward. This means that God uses these temptations—the hard times of life—to train us and spur us forward. When we want to quit, the Holy Spirit inside us tells us what to do. Do we listen? That sharp prick in our hearts that tells us to apologize—do we apologize? That voice telling you to keep going past the liquor store, to lose that person's number, to get into the Bible and find the promises of God—do we listen?

God's Bootcamp involves teaching us to depend on him. If we never faced a battle, we'd never learn to lean on God for strength and protection. From the moment we put our faith in God for salvation, we are to depend on him for everything:

Aren't you glad that God doesn't just throw us into the battle unprepared? He doesn't just say, "Here's a sword, and here's some armor. I hope everything works out for you." Rather, as a good heavenly father, he sovereignly purposes and disposes of all circumstances in our lives so that when the day of battle comes, we are prepared. Furthermore, he has given us not just any sword to take into the fight but rather the Sword of the Spirit, the Word of God.

Prayer: Father, in Jesus' name, I thank You for being my rock and my refuge. Thank You for training me for the battles I face in life. Help me to rely on Your strength and wisdom in every situation. Teach me to trust in Your training process, knowing that You are shaping me into the person You've called me to be. Fill me with Your Spirit and equip me for victory. In Jesus' name, I pray. Amen.

CHAPTER 16

Good Workers

"Work hard so you can present yourself to God and receive his approval. Be a good worker, one who does not need to be ashamed and who correctly explains the word of truth."

2 Timothy 2:15 (NLT)

As **Defenders of the Faith,** we will work hard, give our best, be diligent, present ourselves to God, and receive His approval.

In the apostle Paul's letter to Timothy, he exhorts him to be diligent in his work, especially in correctly explaining the word of truth. This call to diligence applies not only to Timothy but to all believers, urging us to embrace a lifestyle of good works that glorify God. Let's reflect on the importance of this verse and discover how we can apply it to our lives.

First, Paul emphasizes the need to "work hard" in our service to God. As Christ followers, we are called to be active participants in His kingdom work. It's not enough to passively coast through life, expecting blessings and rewards, without investing our time, talents, and energy in fulfilling God's purposes. Diligence is the key that unlocks the door to a life of purpose and impact.

Our motivation for good works must be rooted in a desire to present ourselves to God and receive His approval. Our ultimate goal should not be to seek the approval and praise of men but rather to please our Heavenly Father. When our actions are motivated by a deep love for God, our good works become an act of worship and a reflection of our gratitude for His grace.

Being a "good worker" implies a commitment to excellence in all that we do. Our faith should permeate every area of our lives, including our relationships, careers, and ministries. We are called to be ambassadors of Christ, representing Him well in all circumstances. As we strive for excellence, we honor God and inspire others to pursue goodness and righteousness.

It's important to note that our good works are not a means to earn salvation. We are saved by grace through faith in Jesus Christ alone. Our good works are a response to the transforming power of God's love and a demonstration of our faith. They are evidence of the inner change that occurs when we surrender our lives to Christ. As we allow the Holy Spirit to work in and through us, our good works become a natural outpouring of our love for God and others.

Finally, Paul emphasizes the importance of correctly explaining the word of truth. As Christ followers, we have been entrusted with the precious gospel message. It's our responsibility to handle the Word of God with care, accurately declaring its truth and power. This requires a commitment to study and meditate on Scripture, seeking the guidance of the Holy Spirit to rightly divide the Word.

As Christ followers, we are called to work hard and honor God in all that we do. Our motivation should come from a desire to please God and receive His approval, rather than seeking the applause of men. Let's strive for excellence, understanding that our good works are a response to God's grace and an expression of our faith.

Bob Pritchard says, "The goal of being an approved worker should be the goal of all of God's children. The diligent application of all our energy to the service of God will allow us to join Timothy in standing before God without shame."

Prayer: Father, in Jesus' name, I thank You for the gift of salvation and the opportunity to serve You. Help me to be diligent in my good works, working hard to bring glory to Your name. May my motivations be pure, seeking Your approval rather than the praise of men. Empower me by Your Spirit to be a good worker, exemplifying excellence in all areas of my life. Guide me in correctly explaining Your word so that I may be a faithful steward of the truth. In Jesus' name, I pray. Amen.

CHAPTER 17

Guarding Our Steps

"Guard your steps when you go to the house of God. To draw near to listen is better than to offer the sacrifice of fools, for they do not know that they are doing evil."

Ecclesiastes 5:1 (ESV)

As **Defenders of the Faith,** we live in a society that is hostile toward God and consistently bombards us with hate and negativity regarding the ways and things of God. Because of this, it is essential that we guard our steps.

In the book of Ecclesiastes, we find the wise words of King Solomon, who experienced every pleasure and indulgence the world had to offer. Throughout his life, he came to the realization of the importance of guarding our steps, particularly when we come into the presence of God.

Ecclesiastes 5:1 begins with the admonition to "Guard your steps when you go to the house of God." These words

71

emphasize the significance of approaching God with reverence, humility, and a sincere heart. Just as we walk carefully on dangerous paths, we ought to be mindful of the steps we take when we enter God's presence.

The verse continues, highlighting the purpose behind this caution: "To draw near to listen is better than to offer the sacrifice of fools." Here, we are reminded that the primary reason for coming to the house of God is not to engage in empty rituals or superficial displays of religiosity. Rather, it is to draw near to Him, to listen to His voice, and to seek His wisdom and guidance.

Often, we are tempted to approach our relationship with God in a casual or half-hearted manner. You know, the "God is my best friend attitude." We may find ourselves caught up in the busyness of life, offering God only fragments of our attention and devotion. But the writer of Ecclesiastes urges us to reconsider this approach, reminding us that true worship and connection with God require intentional and wholehearted engagement.

The verse goes on to say, "For they do not know that they are doing evil." It highlights the danger of thoughtless and insincere worship. When we come before God with a careless or distracted mindset, we risk falling into the trap of self-deception. We may fool ourselves into believing that we are fulfilling our spiritual obligations, yet we miss out on the transformative power of a genuine encounter with God.

So, how can we guard our steps and ensure that our worship is authentic and pleasing to God? First, it begins with a humble heart. We must approach God, recognizing His holiness and our unworthiness. This posture of humility allows us to surrender our pride and selfish desires, enabling us to listen and obey.

Secondly, we guard our steps by prioritizing quality over quantity. It is not about the number of words spoken in prayer or the grandeur of our gestures, but rather the depth of our relationship with God. We should strive for intimate communion with Him, taking the time to listen to His voice through prayer, Scripture, and the promptings of the Holy Spirit.

Lastly, guarding our steps involves aligning our actions with our beliefs. It means living out our faith in all areas of our lives, demonstrating the transformation that God's presence brings. As we seek to draw near to Him, may our steps reflect the love, grace, and truth that He embodies.

Ecclesiastes 5:1 serves as a gentle reminder to guard our steps when we approach God. Let's not be fooled by empty sacrifices or superficial religiosity. Instead, let's come before Him with reverence, humility, and a sincere desire to draw near, listen, and obey. May our worship be marked by authenticity, transforming our hearts and lives as we encounter the living God.

Prayer: Father, in Jesus' name, help me to guard my steps as I approach Your presence. May I cultivate reverence, humility, and sincerity in my relationship with you? Guide me along the path of righteousness and deepen my connection with You. In Jesus' name, I pray. Amen.

CHAPTER 18

Holding Firm

"He must hold firm to the trustworthy word as taught, so that he may be able to give instruction in sound doctrine and also to rebuke those who contradict it."
Titus 1:9 (ESV)

As **Defenders of the Faith,** we must consistently be aware that the enemy is always trying to destroy the impact of God's word in our lives. He knows that if he can do that, we will be neutralized in our faith.

Think about it. It can be simple to allow the culture we live in to negatively influence us. The world around us is filled with conflicting messages, making it essential for us, as followers of Christ, to hold firm to the Word of God. In this letter to Titus, the apostle Paul exhorts him to hold firm to the teachings he had received so that he could effectively instruct others and refute false teachings

Holding firm requires a solid foundation, and what better foundation can there be than the Word of God? The Bible is not merely a book of ancient wisdom but a living and active testament to the nature and character of our unchanging God. Through the Scriptures, we gain insight, wisdom, and guidance for every aspect of our lives. It is the unchanging truth in a world that is ever-changing.

When we hold firm to God's Word, we anchor ourselves in truth. We equip ourselves to discern between right and wrong, to navigate the complexities of life, and to make decisions that align with God's will. The Psalmist understood the importance of holding firm when he declared, "I have hidden your word in my heart that I might not sin against you" (Psalm 119:11 NIV). The Word of God is a lamp to our feet and a light to our path (Psalm 119:105), guiding us through life's darkest moments.

Holding firm to God's Word empowers us to stand against false teachings and the lies of the enemy. The apostle Paul warns the Ephesian church about being "tossed to and fro by the waves and carried about by every wind of doctrine" (Ephesians 4:14 ESV). In a world that presents countless philosophies, it's easy to be deceived. But when we are firmly rooted in God's Word, we can discern truth from falsehood, allowing us to stand strong against the waves of false teaching.

In addition to personal growth and discernment, holding firm to God's Word enables us to fulfill our God-given purpose. As Paul instructs Titus, by holding firm to the trustworthy word, he will be able to give instruction in sound doctrine and rebuke those who contradict it. Similarly, when we hold firm to the Word of God, we become equipped to share the truth with others, to encourage and build up fellow believers, and to be a light in the world.

Let's commit ourselves to holding firm to God's Word. Let's study it diligently, meditate on its truth, and apply its teachings to our lives. As we do, we will find strength, wisdom, and direction for our journey of faith. We will be able to stand firm in the face of opposition, and we will impact the world around us with the life-transforming message of Christ.

Prayer: Father, in Jesus' name, help me to hold firm to Your Word. It will be my guide, my anchor, and my source of strength in every season of life. Empower me to discern truth from falsehood and to stand firm against the winds of false teaching. Fill me with a deep hunger for Your Word, so that I may grow in my understanding and application of its truth. In Jesus' name, I pray. Amen.

CHAPTER 19

Honoring Jesus

*"But in your hearts honor Christ the Lord as holy, always
being prepared to make a defense to anyone who asks you
for a reason for the hope that is in you; yet do it with
gentleness and respect.*
1 Peter 3:15 (ESV)

As **Defenders of the Faith,** our objective is to honor our Lord
and Savior Jesus with our lifestyle.

In a world that is increasingly hostile to the message of Christ,
it is essential for us, as Christ followers, to honor Him with
steadfast hearts. The Apostle Peter, writing to the early
believers, encourages them to hold Jesus as holy in their
hearts. This exhortation holds great significance even today,
as it calls us to live our lives in a way that brings honor to our
Lord and Savior.

To honor Christ as holy means recognizing and
acknowledging His divine nature, His sacrificial love, and His

lordship over our lives. It is an attitude of reverence and respect that permeates every aspect of our being. When we honor Jesus in our hearts, it becomes evident in our words, actions, and attitudes. Our lives become a reflection of His love and grace.

Peter goes on to remind us that we should always be prepared to defend the hope that is within us. In a world full of questions and doubts, our lives should be a testimony to the transformative power of Jesus Christ. We should be ready to share the reason for our hope, which is rooted in the unchanging truth of God's Word and the personal relationship we have with our Savior.

However, Peter emphasizes that we must offer this defense with gentleness and respect. Our aim should never be to win arguments or prove ourselves right. Instead, we are called to share the truth with love, compassion, and humility. Our words and actions should mirror the character of Christ, who was full of grace and truth.

When we honor Jesus Christ with a steadfast heart, we become instruments of His love and grace in a broken and hurting world. We have the privilege of being ambassadors for Christ, representing Him in all that we do. Our lives become living testimonies, drawing others to the hope that resides within us.

Honor is not simply an outward expression; it begins in the depths of our hearts. It requires a genuine commitment to living in alignment with the teachings of Jesus, surrendering our will to His, and allowing His Holy Spirit to transform us from the inside out. It means seeking His guidance in every decision, relying on His strength in times of weakness, and displaying His love in our interactions with others.

As we strive to honor Christ in our hearts, let's remember that our faith is not meant to be kept hidden or restricted to our personal lives. It's a faith that is meant to be shared with the world around us. May our lives be a shining example of the hope and joy that can only be found in Jesus Christ.

Prayer: Father, in the name of Jesus, I thank You for the privilege of knowing and following You. Help me to honor

You with a steadfast heart, recognizing Your holiness, and surrendering my life to Your Lordship. Fill me with Your love and compassion, so that I am ready to share the reason for my hope with gentleness and respect. May my life reflect Your grace and truth, drawing others to You. In Jesus' name, I pray. Amen.

CHAPTER 20

Remaining in Christ

"But if you remain in me and my words remain in you,
you may ask for anything you want. and it will be granted!"
John 15:7 (NLT)

As **Defenders of the Faith,** our primary responsibility is to remain in Jesus, which means to remain or dwell.

In John 15:7, Jesus invites us into a profound relationship with Him, one that is built on remaining in Him and allowing His words to dwell richly within us. This verse holds a promise that should ignite our hearts and awaken our spirits to the incredible possibilities that come with a life firmly rooted in Christ.

"Remain" implies steadfastness, an unwavering commitment to abide in Jesus and His teachings. It means we are not influenced by the shifting tides of this world but anchored in the unchanging truth of the Gospel. As we remain in Christ, we find our source of strength, wisdom, and guidance.

Jesus assures us that if we allow His words to abide in us, we have the privilege to approach Him with our requests, and they will be granted. It is a powerful invitation to seek a deep, intimate connection with the Lord, to immerse ourselves in His Word, and to align our desires with His will.

When we remain in Christ, our hearts become aligned with His desires. Our petitions are no longer driven by selfish ambition or personal gain but are rooted in His purposes and plans. Our prayers become an avenue for us to participate in His will on earth as it is in heaven.

Remaining in Christ is not a passive state but an active pursuit. It requires intentional time spent in prayer, studying the Scriptures, and cultivating a vibrant relationship with Him. As we soak in His Word, our minds are renewed, and our spirits are transformed. Our prayers become an overflow of the truth that dwells within us.

In this promise, Jesus is not guaranteeing a "blank check" approach to prayer but rather an invitation to align our desires with His heart. As we remain in Him, His perfect love, wisdom, and sovereignty shape our desires. We begin to see our prayers being answered, not only because we ask according to His will but also because our hearts are attuned to His purposes.

As we meditate on John 15:7, let us be encouraged to deepen our roots in Christ. Let us prioritize spending time in His presence, saturating our minds with His truth, and seeking His guidance in every aspect of our lives. As we do so, we will live the abundant life that Jesus promised—a life filled with heavenly favor, answered prayers, and unwavering joy that is unaffected by external circumstances.

Today, let's embrace the invitation to remain in Christ wholeheartedly. Let's surrender our will, align our desires with His, and cultivate a lifestyle of intimacy with our Savior. Let's remember that when we abide in Him and His words abide in us, we have the privilege of approaching the throne of grace with confidence, knowing that our requests will be heard and answered according to His perfect plan.

Prayer: Father, in the name of Jesus, I thank You for the invitation to remain in Christ. Help me to prioritize my relationship with You above all else and to allow Your Word to dwell richly within me. Align my desires with Your will and teach me to seek Your face in every aspect of my life. I long to experience the abundant life You have promised, marked by answered prayers and divine favor. May my life bring glory to Your name. In Jesus' name, I pray. Amen.

CHAPTER 21

Resisting Temptations

"Submit yourselves, therefore, to God. Resist the devil,
and he will flee from you."

James 4:7 (ESV)

As **Defenders of the Faith,** we submit and humble ourselves before God, knowing that He gives us the power to resist the devil.

You've no doubt learned that on the journey of faith, we encounter temptations that attempt to divert us from the path God has laid before us. These temptations come in many forms, appealing to our desires, pride, and weaknesses. In the face of such trials, the book of James offers a powerful exhortation: "Submit yourselves therefore to God. Resist the devil, and he will flee from you." These words carry profound wisdom, guiding us toward an unwavering faith strengthened with humility and intimacy with our Heavenly Father.

The foundation for resisting temptation is our submission to God. This act of surrender is not a sign of weakness but a display of incredible strength. When we submit to God, we acknowledge His sovereignty and wisdom, recognizing that He alone can guide us through the trials and challenges we face. As we yield our will to His, we align ourselves with His perfect plan, trusting that His ways are higher than our ways.

Now, understand that submitting to God does not guarantee a life free from temptations. On the contrary, it is when we walk on the path of righteousness that the devil intensifies his efforts to deceive and distract us. It's here that James exhorts us to "Resist the devil, and he will flee from you." The ability to resist the devil's schemes stems from the strength we receive when we are connected to God, abiding in His truth, and walking in obedience.

Always remember that humility is a key virtue in resisting temptation. Pride is often the gateway through which temptations gain access to our lives. When we are prideful, we become self-reliant and trust in our own understanding rather than seeking God's guidance. Humility, on the other hand, humbles us before God, recognizing our limitations and dependence on Him. As Proverbs 3:34 (ESV) states, "Toward the scorners, he is scornful, but to the humble, he gives favor." God honors the humble heart and gives strength and wisdom to overcome temptations.

Jesus Christ serves as the ultimate example of resisting temptation. In the wilderness, He faced Satan's temptations, yet He remained steadfast in His submission to God's will. Each time the devil tried to deceive Him, Jesus responded with Scripture, demonstrating the power of God's Word in overcoming temptation. We, too, can wield this powerful weapon against the enemy by meditating on the Scriptures, memorizing them, and internalizing them, so that in times of trial, the Word of God will be our shield and guide.

To resist temptation effectively, we must draw near to God in constant communion. Cultivating a personal relationship with Him through prayer, worship, and study of His Word strengthens our faith and keeps us aligned with His purposes. When we are intimately connected with God, our hearts align with His desires, making it easier to discern and reject the lures of the enemy.

In the face of temptation, let's remember that we are not alone in our struggle. 1 Corinthians 10:13 (ESV) assures us that "No temptation has overtaken you that is not common to man. God is faithful, and he will not let you be tempted beyond your ability, but with the temptation, he will also provide the way of escape, that you may be able to endure it." God is always with us, and His grace empowers us to withstand temptation and walk in righteousness.

Always remember, James 4:7 reminds us that resisting temptation requires submission to God, embracing humility, and drawing near to Him. In our surrender, we find strength, and in humility, we find protection against the enemy's deceit. As we draw closer to God, we discover the abundant grace and wisdom He provides to withstand every trial. Let's stand firm in our faith, trusting in God's unfailing love and relying on His Word as we navigate life's challenges. By doing so, we will find victory in resisting temptation and walking confidently on the path God has ordained for us.

Prayer: Father, in Jesus' name, I thank you that in you I am an overcomer. I will humble myself and submit myself to you, knowing that you will strengthen me to overcome all the temptations the enemy brings into my life. In Jesus' name, I pray. Amen

CHAPTER 22

Standing Firm

"Now I would remind you, brothers, of the gospel I preached to you, which you received, in which you stand, and by which you are being saved if you hold fast to the word I preached to you—unless you believed in vain."

1 Corinthians 15:1-2 (ESV)

In our journey of faith, there are times when the storms of life threaten to shake us, the currents of doubt attempt to pull us away, and the waves of temptation try to push us off course. In the midst of these challenges, God calls us to stand firm in Him, rooted and grounded in the unshakable truth of the Gospel. The apostle Paul, in his letter to the Corinthians, reminds us of the significance of standing firm in the Gospel, for it is through the Gospel that we find salvation, purpose, and unwavering hope.

First, Paul speaks of the importance of remembering the Gospel. He says, "Now I would remind you, brothers, of the gospel I preached to you, which you received." It's easy to become distracted by the cares of this world, the allure of worldly success, or even the pressures of religious legalism. However, as Christ followers, we are called to constantly fix our gaze on the Gospel, for it is the foundation upon which our faith stands. By reminding ourselves daily of the Gospel, we are reminded of God's love, grace, and mercy extended to us through Jesus Christ.

Second, Paul emphasizes that the Gospel is not merely a one-time event but an ongoing process in our lives. He states, "In which you stand and by which you are being saved." The Gospel is not only the door through which we enter into a relationship with God, but it's also the source of our strength and transformation as believers. It is through the Gospel that we receive the power of the Holy Spirit, who empowers us to live lives that are pleasing to God and reflect His love for the world. Standing firm in the Gospel means continually relying on God's grace and allowing His Spirit to work in and through us.

And Paul urges us to hold fast to the word of God, for our faith is not a hollow belief but a steadfast commitment. He says, "If you hold fast to the word I preached to you—unless you believed in vain," the world may tempt us to compromise our convictions or dilute the truth of the Gospel. Yet we are called to stand firm, unwavering in our commitment to God's Word. Holding fast to the Word of God means allowing it to shape our thoughts, guide our actions, and serve as the anchor of our faith. In doing so, we guard against the deceptions of the enemy and remain firmly rooted in God's truth.

As we reflect on Paul's exhortation to stand firm in the Gospel, let's be encouraged and empowered to live out our faith with confidence and conviction. In a world that is constantly changing and uncertain, the Gospel remains an unshakable foundation. May we remember the significance of the Gospel, stand firm in our identity as children of God, and hold fast to His Word, knowing that our salvation, purpose, and hope are found in Christ alone.

Prayer: Father, in Jesus' name, I thank You for the precious gift of the Gospel. Help me to constantly remind myself of its truth and significance in my life. Empower me by Your Spirit to stand firm in the midst of trials, doubts, and temptations. Give me the grace to hold fast to Your Word and to live out my faith with conviction. My life will be a reflection of Your love, grace, and truth to the world around me. In Jesus' name, I pray. Amen.

CHAPTER 23

Steadfast in Trials

"Blessed is the man who remains steadfast under trial, for when he has stood the test, he will receive the crown of life, which God has promised to those who love him."
James 1:12 (ESV)

As **Defenders of the Faith**, we understand that we will face trials and hardships. But as James writes, to be blessed, we must remain steadfast when we experience them. And when we do, we'll receive the crown of life that the Lord has promised those who love Him.

As you know, life is a journey filled with peaks and valleys, with moments of joy and moments of sorrow. As Christ followers, we are not exempt from trials and challenges. In fact, the Bible assures us that we will face various trials in this world. However, James reminds us that there is a great reward for those who remain steadfast through it all—the crown of life.

Here's what it means to be o be steadfast: to have unwavering faith and determination, even in the face of adversity. It's not a passive attitude toward our circumstances but an active decision to trust in God's goodness and power regardless of what comes our way. The verse tells us that the one who remains steadfast under trial is blessed. This blessing is not the absence of difficulties, but rather the presence of God's grace and favor in the midst of them.

Remember, Jesus Himself warned His disciples that in this world they would have trouble, but He also encouraged them to take heart because He had overcome the world (John 16:33). As Christ followers, we are called to have the same spirit of steadfastness that Jesus demonstrated throughout His earthly life. His unwavering commitment to the Father's will, even in the face of betrayal, suffering, and death, serves as the ultimate example for us.

You see, remaining steadfast under trial involves holding onto our faith in God and His promises. When we face challenges, it's easy to question God's plan or doubt His love for us. So, always remember, the Bible reassures us that God is always with us and that He works all things together for the good of those who love Him (Romans 8:28). As we stand firm in our faith, we cultivate a deeper dependence on God and experience His overcoming power in times of difficulty.

Being steadfast in trials also involves perseverance in prayer. When we encounter hardships, we are encouraged to bring our burdens and concerns before the Lord. Prayer keeps us connected to God and reminds us of His faithfulness. Through prayer, we can find the strength to endure and experience peace that surpasses all understanding (Philippians 4:6-7).

As we live through trials with steadfastness, we must also remember that God is using these challenges to refine our character and strengthen our faith. Just as gold is purified through fire, our faith is tested in the middle of trials. The apostle Peter writes in 1 Peter 1:7, "So that the tested genuineness of your faith—more precious than gold that perishes though it is tested by fire—may be found to result in praise, glory, and honor at the revelation of Jesus Christ."

So, in times of difficulty, it's crucial to surround ourselves with a community of believers who can support and encourage us.

The body of Christ is designed to uplift one another and bear each other's burdens (Galatians 6:2). When we face trials together, we experience the love and care of God through the actions of fellow believers.

Always remember, James 1:12 reminds us that steadfastness under trial leads to a blessed reward—the crown of life. Being steadfast does not mean we will never struggle, but it means we hold firm to our faith and trust in God's goodness and faithfulness through all circumstances. As we face trials with unwavering faith, perseverance in prayer, and the support of a Christ-centered community, we grow in our relationship with God and become more like Christ. Let's, embrace trials as opportunities for growth and rejoice in the promise of the crown of life that awaits those who remain steadfast in love for Him.

Prayer: Father, in the name of Jesus, I thank you that you have a great reward for me, and that is the crown of life. I will be diligent to read your word, memorize it, and worship you so that I will be empowered to overcome the enemy. Thank you for Your unconditional love. In Jesus' name, I pray. Amen

CHAPTER 24

Surrounded

"Therefore, since we are surrounded by so great a cloud of witnesses, let us also lay aside every weight and sin which clings so closely, and let us run with endurance the race that is set before us."
Hebrews 12:1 (ESV)

As **Defenders of the Faith,** a great cloud of witnesses who have come before us and are encouraging us to run the race of faith are all around us.

Life is full of challenges and obstacles that often make us feel weary and burdened. We may encounter discouragement, doubts, and the weight of our own mistakes and shortcomings. However, the author of Hebrews reminds us that there is a large cloud of witnesses all around us, despite the trials. These witnesses are not merely bystanders; rather, they are people who have come before us and have demonstrated faith and tenacity.

When we think of being surrounded, we might imagine a tight, suffocating space, but the imagery presented in Hebrews 12:1 is quite the opposite. The cloud of witnesses envelops us, forming a supportive and encouraging presence. It's a spiritual community that cheers us on as we navigate the challenges of life's race.

The cloud of witnesses includes biblical heroes like Abraham, Moses, David, and Elijah, among others. These men and women faced their own share of trials, yet they overcame them through their faith in God. Their stories remind us that we are not alone in our struggles. They assure us that God is faithful and that His grace is sufficient to sustain us through every difficulty.

To fully embrace the encouragement and inspiration of this cloud of witnesses, we are called to lay aside two things: "every weight" and "sin which clings so closely." These hindrances can impede our progress in the race set before us. They can drain our energy, distract our focus, and create stumbling blocks on our journey of faith.

Weight refers to anything that weighs us down—be it excessive worry, fear, self-doubt, material possessions, or unhealthy relationships. We are encouraged to cast off these burdens, surrendering them to God, who promises to carry our heavy loads and provide rest for our souls (Matthew 11:28–30).

Sin is another obstacle that can entangle us and hinder our spiritual growth. It's essential to recognize that the cloud of witnesses is not a gathering of perfect people but individuals who experienced forgiveness and restoration. By confessing our sins to God, seeking His forgiveness, and repenting, we can break free from the chains of sin and experience the freedom and victory found in Jesus Christ.

Once we have laid aside these weights and sins, we are then ready to run the race with endurance. Endurance implies persistence, perseverance, and unwavering commitment. It means embracing the challenges and knowing that God is with us and that His strength sustains us. When we fix our eyes on Jesus, who is the author and perfecter of our faith (Hebrews 12:2), we find the motivation, strength, and guidance to keep moving forward.

The cloud of witnesses serves as a reminder that we are part of a greater story—a story of faith, hope, and redemption. Their lives bear witness to God's faithfulness, and they encourage us to press on. They cheer for us, urging us to keep our focus on Jesus, who is the ultimate example of endurance and victory.

Let's not lose sight of the fact that there is a sizable cloud of witnesses all around us. Their stories remind us of God's faithfulness and encourage us to persevere in our own race of faith. As we lay aside the weights and sins that hinder us, let's fix our eyes on Jesus, the One who empowers us to endure and overcome. May His grace strengthen us today, and may we, in turn, become witnesses to those who will come after us.

Prayer: Father, in Jesus' name, I thank You for surrounding me with a great cloud of witnesses who inspire and encourage me in my faith journey. Help me to cast off every weight and sin that hinders me and give me the endurance to run the race with perseverance. I fix my eyes on Jesus, who is my source of strength and an example of faith. In Jesus' name, I pray. Amen.

CHAPTER 25

The Bond of Friendship

"You adulterous people! Do you not know that friendship
with the world is enmity with God? Therefore, whoever
wishes to be a friend of the world makes himself
an enemy of God."
James 4:4 (ESV)

As **Defenders of the Faith**, we will be intentional about nurturing godly friendships that sharpen and strengthen our faith. We will also remember to be godly friends to others, offering love, support, and guidance rooted in Christ.

In a world filled with constant change and uncertainty, finding true and lasting friendships can be a challenge. We often seek companionship, looking for someone who understands us, accepts us, and walks alongside us through the ups and downs of life. However, as Christ followers, we are called to a higher standard of friendship—a friendship that goes beyond mere worldly connections.

James, in his letter, reminds us of the importance of discerning our alliances and friendships. He boldly declares, "You adulterous people! Do you not know that friendship with the world is enmity with God?" (James 4:4 ESV). These words may initially sound harsh, but they serve as a wake-up call for us to evaluate the nature of our relationships and the influences they have on our spiritual journey.

The world presents us with attractions and distractions that can easily entangle us. It entices us with temporary pleasures, false promises, and superficial connections. But as children of God, we are called to live in the world without being of the world. Our friendships should reflect this distinction. We are called to be set apart and to choose godly friendships that uplift, encourage, and draw us closer to Jesus.

True friendship, as exemplified by Christ Himself, is grounded in love, loyalty, and sacrificial giving. Jesus says, "Greater love has no one than this, that someone lay down his life for his friends" (John 15:13 ESV). He showed us the depth of His love by laying down His life on the cross, not only for His disciples but for all who would believe in Him. This selfless act serves as a reminder of the kind of friendship we should strive to cultivate.

Godly friendships should reflect the character of Christ. They are built on trust, honesty, and a shared pursuit of God's will. These friendships uplift us, challenge us to grow in our faith, and help us navigate the complexities of life. They celebrate our victories and stand by us in our darkest moments. A godly friend is one who speaks truth in love, encourages us to stay aligned with God's Word, and gently corrects us when we veer off course.

While it's essential to seek godly friendships, we must also be cautious of the world's influence. James warns that friendship with the world leads to enmity with God. When we prioritize worldly values and conform to their patterns, we distance ourselves from God and His perfect plan for our lives. We must guard our hearts and minds, being discerning in our choices and associations, so that we do not compromise our faith.

Today, let's reflect on our friendships and evaluate their impact on our spiritual walk. Are our friends drawing us closer to God or leading us away? Are we being intentional about nurturing godly friendships that sharpen and strengthen our faith? Let's also remember to be godly friends to others, offering love, support, and guidance rooted in Christ.

Prayer: Father, in Jesus' name, I thank You for the gift of friendship. Help me discern the relationships in my life and choose friends who will lead me closer to You. Give me the strength to let go of unhealthy friendships and cultivate godly friendships that reflect Your love. My friendships will be a testimony of Your grace and truth in my life. In Jesus' name, I pray. Amen.

CHAPTER 26

The Good Fight of Faith

"Fight the good fight of faith. Take hold of the eternal life to which you were called and about which you made the good confession in the presence of many witnesses."
1 Timothy 6:12 (ESV)

As **Defenders of the Faith,** we are called to fight the good fight of faith. Contrary to what you might think, there is such a thing as a good fight. It's a good fight because we win!

In the spiritual journey of every believer, there are battles to be fought. Challenges, trials, and temptations arise and try to hinder our progress and weaken our faith. However, God's Word encourages us to "fight the good fight of the faith." These words from the apostle Paul to Timothy hold timeless significance and provide us with valuable insights into the nature of our spiritual warfare.

The good fight of faith is not a physical battle with visible adversaries; it's a spiritual warfare fought in the realm of our hearts, minds, and souls. The enemy seeks to undermine our trust in God, sow seeds of doubt, and distract us from the path of righteousness. Yet, as followers of Christ, we have been equipped with spiritual armor (Ephesians 6:10–18) and empowered by the Holy Spirit to stand firm and overcome.

The good fight of faith requires determination to persevere despite the challenges we will encounter. It calls us to remain steadfast in our beliefs, unwavering in our commitment to God's truth, and unyielding in our pursuit of righteousness. It's not a fight we wage in our own strength but one in which we rely on God's power and guidance.

To fight the good fight of faith effectively, we must first receive the eternal life to which we have been called. Our salvation is not merely a one-time event but an ongoing relationship with the living God. We must continually deepen our understanding of God's character, His promises, and His will for our lives through prayer, Bible study, and fellowship. As we grow in intimacy with our Heavenly Father, we become better equipped to face the challenges that come our way.

In this fight, we are not striving for victory but fighting from a position of victory. Jesus Christ has already conquered sin, death, and the powers of darkness through His sacrificial death and resurrection. We are more than conquerors in Him (Romans 8:37). Even in the face of adversity, we can confidently press on, knowing that the battle has already been won.

Finally, the good fight of faith is not just about our personal spiritual growth; it's also about advancing the kingdom of God. We fight not only for ourselves but also for those who have yet to experience the power of Christ's love. Our victories in the good fight of faith serve as a testimony to the world, drawing others to the hope and salvation found in Jesus.

As we reflect on these words from Paul to Timothy, let's be encouraged to fight the good fight of faith with determination, reliance on God's strength, and a firm grasp on the eternal life to which we have been called. Let's draw strength from the witnesses who have gone before us and motivation from the assurance of victory in Christ. And may our good fight of faith not only transform our lives but also impact the lives of others as we shine the light of God's truth in a world that desperately needs it.

Prayer: Father, in Jesus' name, I thank you for providing victory through the death, burial, and resurrection of Your Son Jesus. Because of this, I am able to fight the good fight of faith in all areas of my life. In Jesus' name, I pray. Amen

CHAPTER 27

The Shield of Faith

"In all circumstances, take up the shield of faith, with which you can extinguish all the flaming darts of the evil one."
Ephesians 6:16 (ESV)

As **Defenders of the Faith,** we must know and use the various weapons that the Lord has given us to defeat the enemy, and one of the primary weapons is the shield of faith.

In the spiritual battle we face each day, always remember that you are not defenseless. God equips us with spiritual armor to withstand the schemes of the enemy. One vital piece of this armor is the shield of faith. Just as a physical shield protects a soldier from incoming arrows or blows, our faith acts as a shield, safeguarding us from the fiery darts of the evil one.

The apostle Paul urges believers to "take up the shield of faith in all circumstances." Notice that he doesn't say "in some circumstances" or "in certain situations." No, he emphasizes the importance of faith as an all-encompassing defense, regardless of the challenges we face. Whether we find ourselves in the midst of trials, temptations, or spiritual attacks, faith becomes our shield.

When we speak of faith, we are not referring to a mere intellectual assent to a set of doctrines or beliefs. True faith goes beyond intellectual knowledge; it is a deeply rooted trust in God's character and His promises. Faith is an unwavering confidence in the goodness, sovereignty, and faithfulness of our Heavenly Father. It is the firm conviction that He is who He says He is and will do what He says He will do.

Just as a soldier trains with his shield to become skilled at deflecting attacks, we too must cultivate and strengthen our faith. This comes through a consistent relationship with God, immersing ourselves in His Word, prayer, and fellowship with other believers. As we grow in our understanding of God's nature, our faith expands, enabling us to trust Him more fully in every situation.

The enemy, who seeks to steal, kill, and destroy, employs various tactics to undermine our faith. He hurls fiery darts of doubt, fear, discouragement, and temptation, aiming to pierce our hearts and weaken our trust in God. But with the shield of faith, we can extinguish these flaming arrows. As we hold firm to our trust in God, His promises, and His character, the enemy's attacks lose their power and impact.

Faith reminds us of God's faithfulness throughout history and in our own lives. It strengthens us to persevere in the face of adversity, knowing that God is with us and that He will never leave us or forsake us. Faith empowers us to stand firm on His Word, which is unchanging and eternal. Faith assures us that nothing is impossible with God and that He works all things together for the good of those who love Him.

Today, let's take up the shield of faith without hesitation. When doubts attack us, when fear tries to paralyze us, when circumstances seem overwhelming, let's remember that we have a shield that cannot be penetrated—the shield of unwavering faith in our Almighty God. As we trust Him and His promises, our faith will serve as a protective barrier against the attacks of the evil one, enabling us to walk in victory and experience the fullness of life God intends for us.

Prayer: Father, in the name of Jesus, I thank You for the gift of faith and for equipping me with the shield that protects me from the enemy's attacks. Help me to deepen my trust in You and Your promises. Strengthen my faith so that I will stand firm in the face of trials, temptations, and doubts. My life be a testament to Your faithfulness. In Jesus' name, I pray, Amen.

CHAPTER 28

The Source of Strength

"God arms me with strength, and he makes my way perfect."
Psalms 18:32 (NLT)

As **Defenders of the Faith**, we understand that we are going to face trials, challenges, and struggles. As we draw near to God, He will give us the strength to persevere.

As you know, life confronts us with challenges, trials, and struggles that can leave us feeling weak, vulnerable, and overwhelmed. We will face circumstances that stretch us to our limits, testing our physical, emotional, and spiritual strength. In such moments, it's essential to remember that our true source of strength lies in God alone. Psalm 18:32 reminds us of this profound truth: "God arms me with strength, and he makes my way perfect."

In this verse, David declares the empowering presence of God in his life. He acknowledges that it's God who equips him with the strength to overcome any obstacle and achieve victory. Just as a soldier relies on his armor to defend himself, David recognizes that his strength comes from God, who provides him with the spiritual armor necessary to face life's battles.

God desires to strengthen us, to fortify us in our weakness, and to make our way perfect. He doesn't promise a life free from difficulties, but He assures us that He will be with us every step of the way. When we face challenges, we can take comfort in knowing that God is right there, ready to empower us.

Strength is not always about physical might or endurance but often relates to our inner being, our resilience, and our ability to stand firm in the face of adversity. God strengthens us from the inside out, giving us the determination, courage, and perseverance we need to navigate life's challenges successfully. When we feel weak, we can turn to Him in prayer and seek His strength, knowing that His power is made perfect in our weakness (2 Corinthians 12:9).

I'm glad God's strength is not limited to our own abilities. He enables us to accomplish more than we could ever imagine by working through us. When we humble ourselves before Him, surrendering our fears and weaknesses, He fills us with His divine power. It is in our reliance on God's strength that we find the assurance that we can do all things through Christ who strengthens us (Philippians 4:13).

As we meditate on Psalms 18:32, let's remember that God's strength is available to us at all times. We don't have to face life's challenges alone. In fact, we were never meant to. We can find comfort in knowing that our heavenly Father is ready to arm us with strength and guide us along the perfect path He has set before us.

Today, whatever trials or difficulties you may be facing, remember that your strength does not lie in your own abilities but in God's unwavering power. Seek Him in prayer, lean on His promises, and trust that He will provide you with the strength you need to overcome every obstacle. With God by your side, you can face any challenge with confidence, knowing that His strength will carry you through.

Prayer: Father, in Jesus' name, I thank You for the assurance that You are my source of strength. Help me to remember that I can rely on Your power and not my own. Fill me with Your Holy Spirit, equipping me to face the challenges that come my way. Give me the courage, resilience, and determination to stand firm in my faith and trust in You. In Jesus' name, I pray. Amen.

CHAPTER 29

Walking in Wisdom

"Walk in wisdom toward outsiders, making the
best use of the time."
Colossians 4:5 (ESV)

As **Defenders of the Faith,** we need to live wise lives toward those who are unbelievers.

As Christ followers, our walk with God extends beyond our private devotions and Sunday worship. It includes every aspect of our lives, including our interactions with others and how we utilize the time God has given us. In Colossians 4:5, the Apostle Paul encourages the Colossian believers, and us as well, to walk in wisdom toward outsiders and make the best use of our time.

To "walk in wisdom" is to live intentionally and discerningly, seeking God's guidance in every step we take. It means allowing His truth and principles to shape our thoughts,

120

actions, and decisions. As we interact with those outside the faith, we are called to demonstrate wisdom in our words, attitudes, and conduct. Our behavior should reflect the transforming power of Christ, drawing others to Him through our love, kindness, and humility.

Walking in wisdom also includes making the best use of the time we have been given. Time is a precious and finite resource. Each passing moment presents us with opportunities to impact lives, share the Gospel, and bring glory to God. Therefore, we are called to be intentional in our actions and seize these opportunities for His Kingdom.

Often, we can get caught up in the busyness of life, neglecting to prioritize what truly matters. We become preoccupied with trivial matters, entertainment, or pursuing our own ambitions while neglecting the eternal significance of our time. However, when we walk in wisdom, we recognize the brevity of life and the urgency of sharing the love of Christ with others.

Walking in wisdom involves seeking God's guidance and direction in our daily decisions. It means aligning our priorities with His will and purpose. We can ask ourselves, "Am I using my time and resources in ways that honor God and bless others?" When we prioritize prayer, Bible study, and spending time in His presence, we position ourselves to receive divine wisdom and discernment.

Walking in wisdom requires a heart of compassion and a willingness to step outside our comfort zones. It involves actively engaging with those who do not yet know Christ and understanding their needs, struggles, and questions. Instead of isolating ourselves from the world, we are called to be salt and light, sharing the hope and truth found in Jesus Christ.

In our interactions with outsiders, we must remember that wisdom is not synonymous with argumentation or forceful persuasion. Rather, it involves listening attentively, respecting different perspectives, and responding with grace and love. Our actions should exemplify Christ's character, allowing His light to shine through us and drawing others closer to Him.

As we walk in wisdom, we must also be mindful of our own spiritual growth. Continual growth in our relationship with God enables us to discern His will more clearly and navigate life's complexities with wisdom and grace. Through regular prayer, studying His Word, and fellowship with other believers, we deepen our understanding of God's truth and cultivate a heart that reflects His wisdom.

Let's commit ourselves to walking in wisdom, seeking God's guidance in every step, and making the best use of the time He has given us. May our lives be a testimony of His love, grace, and transformative power, drawing others to experience the richness of a relationship with Jesus Christ.

Prayer: Father, in Jesus' name, I thank You for Your Word that guides and instructs me in wisdom. Help me to walk in wisdom toward outsiders, making the best use of the time You have given me. Give me discernment and understanding as I interact with those who do not yet know You. Fill me with Your love, compassion, and grace so that I will be an effective ambassador for Your Kingdom. My life will reflect Your wisdom and draw others to Your saving grace. In Jesus' name, I pray. Amen.

CHAPTER 30

We Are His House

"But Christ is faithful over God's house as a son. And we are his house if indeed we hold fast our confidence and our boasting in our hope."
Hebrews 3:6 (ESV)

As **Defenders of the Faith,** we are called to speak this hope boldly, to say it loudly, and to sing it with celebration, knowing this good news has nothing to do with anything we have done and everything to do with the boundless grace that God has bestowed upon us.

In the book of Hebrews, the author describes the superiority of Jesus Christ over all other figures and institutions. In Hebrews 3:6, the author reminds us that Christ is faithful over God's house, and we, as Christ followers, are part of that house. It is an important truth that we need to deeply understand and embrace: we are His house.

God's house in the Old Testament was a physical structure, the temple, where His presence dwelt among His people. However, in the New Testament, with the coming of Jesus Christ, a remarkable transformation took place. Jesus, as the Son of God, fulfilled the role of the temple and became the ultimate dwelling place of God among His people. But that's not all; the amazing truth is that we, as believers, are now considered His house and His dwelling place.

As Christ followers, we have become the dwelling place of God's Spirit. The Holy Spirit now lives within us, transforming our hearts and renewing our minds. We are no longer distant or separated from God; He has chosen to reside within us. This truth should fill us with awe and reverence.

Being God's house means that we are the recipients of His grace, love, and mercy. It means that His presence is with us wherever we go, guiding and leading us on our journey of faith. It means that we are called to be holy, for God dwells within us. We have been set apart for His purposes and called to reflect His character and love in the world around us.

Yet, being His house also carries a responsibility. The verse says, "If indeed we hold fast our confidence and our boasting in our hope," Our faith is not a one-time decision but a continuous, active commitment. We must hold fast to our confidence in Christ and boast in the hope we have in Him. We are to live in a way that brings honor and glory to God, displaying His love, grace, and truth to the lost and dying world around us.

Sometimes, we may find ourselves struggling to hold onto that confidence and hope. Life's challenges, trials, and temptations can shake our faith. However, we must remember that we are not alone on this journey. Christ, who is faithful over God's house, is also faithful to us. He will never leave us or forsake us. He is the anchor for our souls and the source of our strength and encouragement.

Let's remind ourselves daily of the incredible privilege it is to be His house. Let's cultivate an atmosphere of worship, prayer, and intimacy with God in our lives. Let's be vessels through which His love and grace flow freely. May our lives reflect the goodness and glory of the One who dwells within us.

Take a moment to meditate on the truth that you are God's house. Embrace the privilege and responsibility that come with it. Let His presence and love shine through you as you go about your day, knowing that you are a dwelling place for the Most High God.

Prayer: Father, in Jesus' name, I thank you for choosing me to be your dwelling place. Help me to hold fast to the confidence I have in you and to boast in the hope that my life will be a testimony of your love and grace to those around me. In Jesus' name, I pray. Amen.

CHAPTER 31

Witnesses

"You are my witnesses," declares the Lord, "and my servant whom I have chosen, that you may know and believe me and understand that I am he. Before me, no god was formed, nor shall there be any after me.
Isaiah 43:10 (ESV)

As **Defenders of the Faith**, we are His witnesses and called to serve God and testify of His greatness and love. What an amazing calling!

Jesus told His followers before He ascended to heaven that they would be His witnesses. "Here's the knowledge you need: you will receive power when the Holy Spirit comes on you. And you will be My witnesses, first here in Jerusalem, then beyond to Judea and Samaria, and finally to the farthest places on earth." Acts 1:8 (VOICE)

Acts 1:8 emphasizes two things we need to know: 1) The Holy Spirit empowers disciples, and 2) Spirit-filled disciples witness Jesus around the world.

How are we witnesses of Him? What Jesus said to them, he also says to us. We are on earth so we would be his witnesses. In heaven, there will be no witnesses, because in heaven, seeing is believing. There the Lamb will be the light, and he will need no lesser lights, but in this dark world, we are the only light he has. On earth, we are his witnesses. He does not send angels to proclaim his name, and he does not write the gospel in lightning across the skies. He uses people like us to convince other people like us to believe in him. We are God's witnesses.

Take a look at these Scriptures regarding being a witness:

Acts 2:32: God has raised this Jesus to life, and we are all witnesses of the fact.

Acts 3:15: You killed the author of life, but God raised him from the dead. We are witnesses to this.

Acts 10:39–40: We are witnesses of everything he did in the country of the Jews and in Jerusalem. They killed him by hanging him on a tree, but God raised him from the dead on the third day and caused him to be seen.

Acts 13:30–31: But God raised him from the dead, and for many days he was seen by those who had traveled with him from Galilee to Jerusalem. They are now his witnesses to our people.

If we take all these verses together, we can sum them up this way: A witness is a person who tells the truth about Jesus Christ. The disciples testified to the things they knew to be true about Jesus Christ. And, above all else, they testified to the truth of the resurrection.

One of the great generals of the faith said this: "Great faith is the product of great fights. Great testimonies are the outcome of great tests. Great triumphs can only come out of great trials." ~ Smith Wigglesworth

Prayer: Father, in Jesus' name, I thank You for choosing me to be Your witness in the world. Give me the wisdom, boldness, and compassion to effectively bear witness to Your love, grace, and truth. May my life reflect Your character, drawing others to experience the abundant life found in Jesus Christ. Equip me to be a faithful and obedient servant, empowered by Your Spirit to make a lasting impact for Your kingdom. In Jesus' name, I pray. Amen.

You Can Have Eternal Peace
Receive Jesus as Your Personal Savior

The most important relationship for every one of us is our relationship with Jesus Christ. Choosing to believe that he is who he claimed to be—the Son of God and the only way to salvation—and receiving him by faith as your Lord and Savior is the most vital act anyone will ever do. We want life. He is life. We need cleansing. He is the living water.

If you have not yet given your life to Jesus and would like to invite him into your life, here is a simple prayer for you to pray:

Jesus, I believe you are the Son of God, that you died on the cross to rescue me from sin and death and to restore me to the Father. I choose now to turn from my sins, my self-centeredness, and every part of my life that does not please you. I choose you. I give myself to you. I receive your forgiveness and ask you to take your rightful place in my life as my Savior and Lord. Come reign in my heart, fill me with your love and your life, and help me to become a person who is truly loving—a person like you. Restore me, Jesus. Live in me. Love through me. Thank you, God. In Jesus' name, I pray. Amen.

I, _____, have repented of my sin, recognizing God loves me, and that Jesus died, was buried, and rose again. I have received the forgiveness of God and have asked Jesus to be my savior and am now born again this date: _____.

If you have prayed this prayer, I am excited for you and would love to know. Please send me an email to let me know you received Jesus as your personal savior.

FOLLOW US ON
OUR SOCIAL MEDIA
PLATFORMS
SEARCH
@PASTORJNEVILLE

CHURCH:
@PRAISECHAPELCF

WWW.PRAISECHAPELCF.COM

Made in the USA
Las Vegas, NV
06 August 2023

75743339R00075